A Fresh Approach
to Sight-Singing

Joining the Dots
Singing

Grade 2

Alan Bullard

ABRSM

To the Teacher

Joining the Dots Singing offers a wealth of material to help build skill and confidence in sight-singing. Used as part of regular lessons and practice, it will help pupils learn to read new music more quickly and easily, and develop their awareness of rhythm, pitch and other general musicianship skills.

This book is designed to prepare pupils for the sight-singing section of the ABRSM Grade 2 Singing exam, but it will also help instrumentalists to develop their sight-singing skills. While every teacher will have their own approach, pupils who tackle the material in order will – with your help and with regular practice – acquire a sound sight-singing technique.

Each book in the series contains the following mix of technical and creative activities and songs to sing:

Workouts build, step by step, the rhythm and pitch skills required for the grade, and are taught both aurally and from the page. This book helps pupils to distinguish between three and four beats in the bar and introduces dotted rhythms and upward leaps of a 3rd within the tonic triad. The focus of each Workout is identified in a header and then introduced in a 'singing back' exercise for teacher and pupil (if necessary, you could improvise more). A number of short exercises promote effective reading of staff notation using tonic sol-fa, numbered degrees of the scale or any suitable syllable.

Make Music provides an opportunity for pupils to build performing confidence in and through creative and imaginative work. Using an approach that is not primarily notation-based, the activities here will help to familiarize pupils with the 'feel' of a key-centre and the way that pitches relate to it, and to develop their sense of rhythm. You and your pupils can approach these exercises together in whatever way you find most comfortable, perhaps with some trial and error – experimenting is a good way to learn here!

It Takes Two enables two pupils (or pupil and teacher) to work together on the techniques learnt, and to build confidence in singing an independent part using rounds. It also offers the opportunity to practise singing with a piano accompaniment. Your pupils should take as long as necessary preparing the pieces as outlined. Plenty of time taken here, together with lots of practice, will help them to focus on the salient points in an exam sight-singing test, with its shorter preparation time.

Read and Sing provides an invaluable source of sight-singing material for those preparing for the Grade 2 Singing exam. The songs are intended to be sung at sight or after a short practice time, with the focus on keeping going. Each one has a title (unlike those in the exam), and they sometimes have a slightly wider range of colour and detail in the accompaniment, to help pupils reflect the musical mood suggested by the title. To replicate an exam scenario, encourage your pupils to set a tempo they can maintain and follow this in the accompaniment, helping to keep the song going. Some of the Read and Sing material is also provided in the bass clef, for those who wish to develop fluency in reading both clefs. (All the treble-clef material may also be sung an octave lower.)

Songs with Words, the final page, consists of two short songs to learn. The first is a round – enabling several pupils to sing independently – and the second is a song with piano accompaniment. As these are designed to be learnt, they push the boundaries slightly while employing the same rhythms and intervals as the material in the rest of the book.

First published in 2015 by ABRSM (Publishing) Ltd,
a wholly owned subsidiary of ABRSM,
4 London Wall Place, London EC2Y 5AU, United Kingdom
Reprinted in 2017

© 2015 by The Associated Board of the Royal Schools of Music

AB 3822

Illustrations by Willie Ryan, www.illustrationweb.com/willieryan

Book design and cover by www.adamhaystudio.com

Music and text origination by Julia Bovee

Printed in England by Halstan & Co. Ltd, Amersham, Bucks., on materials from sustainable sources

Dear Singer,

Joining the Dots will help you to sing music from notation and learn new songs more quickly and easily.

In this book you will find lots of ideas to help with the Grade 2 Singing exam and with your sight-singing generally. You will find it best if you work through the book from beginning to end, with your teacher's help.

There are several different things to do:

Workouts to develop your sense of rhythm and pitch

Make Music in which you can explore musical ideas

It Takes Two – music to sing with another singer or a pianist

Read and Sing where there are a number of short songs to sing – read the title to set the mood, work out the rhythm, find the notes and, when you're ready, sing the song right through without stopping!

On the last page of the book you'll find **Songs with Words**, featuring two songs for you to learn.

Enjoy singing, and enjoy Joining the Dots!

Alan Bullard

Contents

Workout 1 $\frac{4}{4}$

Copy the rhythm

- Echo this rhythm with your teacher by singing back each phrase in time, without looking at the music
- Your teacher will count in two bars before starting
- You can both tap the beat throughout

Rhythm

Here are some rhythms in 4/4 time (four crotchet beats in each bar).

- Sing these phrases to any suitable syllable while tapping the beat (or pulse)
- Find the starting note, with your teacher's help if needed
- Remember to take a breath during the crotchet rest in the middle – but keep tapping the beat!

Workout 2

New key:
D major

Singing back

- Make a tune with your teacher by echoing each phrase in time, without looking at the music
- Your teacher will play you the key-chord and first note, and count in two bars
- You can both tap the beat throughout
- The option is given for singing to numbers or to tonic sol-fa

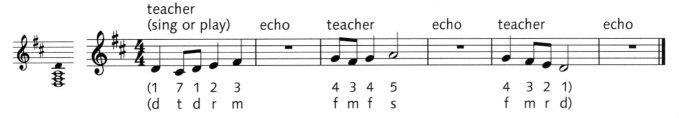

Rhythm and notes

Rhythm and notes, together, are the essential starting point of singing a tune. Always focus on these two elements one by one, and then put them both together. This book introduces the new key of **D major**, and all the tunes begin and end on the 1st note of the scale (the key-note, or 'doh').

- Check the key signature, and listen to the key-chord and starting note
- Sing the rhythm on the starting note only, while tapping the beat
- Then sing all the notes (or pitches) in free time
- Lastly, put rhythm and notes together, tapping the beat quietly throughout

Workout 3

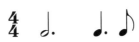

Copy the rhythm

- Echo this rhythm with your teacher by singing back each phrase in time, without looking at the music
- Your teacher will count in two bars before starting
- You can both tap the beat throughout

Rhythm

The rhythms on this page now include dotted notes.

- Sing these phrases to any suitable syllable while tapping the beat
- Find the starting note, with your teacher's help if needed
- Remember to take a breath during the crotchet rest in the middle – but keep tapping the beat!

Workout 4

Singing back

- Make a tune with your teacher by echoing each phrase in time, without looking at the music
- Your teacher will play you the key-chord and first note, and count in two bars
- You can both tap the beat throughout

Rhythm and notes

These tunes in 4/4 time are in several different keys, always starting and ending on the key-note.

- Check the key signature, and listen to the key-chord and starting note
- Sing the rhythm on the starting note only, while tapping the beat
- Then sing all the notes in free time
- Lastly, put rhythm and notes together, tapping the beat quietly throughout

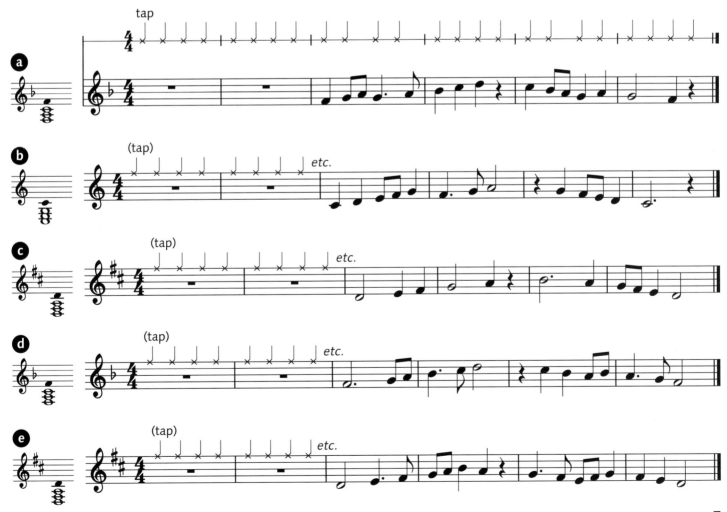

Make Music

Bicycle Ride

Make a song to fit the words below:
- First, say the words out loud to make a rhythm in 4/4 time
- Now make it into a song in the key of F major

Pedals turning, wheels whirling, down the hill with brakes burning!

Early Morning Stroll

- Sing this rhythm on the note D several times, to any syllable
- Now make the rhythm into a tune in the key of D major
- Note the new dynamic, *mf* (moderately loud)

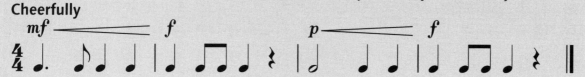

It Takes Two

Here are two duets to sing with your teacher or another pupil, followed by three pages of songs for voice and piano. You can sing these using any suitable syllable.

Cloudless Landscape

- Check the time signature, tempo and key signature, and listen to the key-chord and starting note
- Sing the rhythm on the starting note, counting in two bars before you start (you can do this together)
- On your own, sing the notes in free time and then combine rhythm and notes – then sing the duet together

Ebb and Flow

- In this round, you both sing the same music – practise the rhythm first and then the notes
- Voice 2 starts when Voice 1 reaches the ✳ sign
- Repeat several times, if you wish

It Takes Two (continued)

Prepare *In the Shadows* like this:
- Check the time signature, tempo and key signature, and listen to the key-chord and starting note
- Sing the rhythm on the starting note only, while tapping the beat

- Then sing all the notes in free time – repeat until you are sure that they are right

- Now put rhythm and notes together
- Follow the expression marks to give the phrases a delicate musical shape, noting the new dynamic, **mp** (moderately quiet)
- When you are ready to sing with the piano, listen again to the key-chord and starting note, and tap two bars before you start – keep tapping quietly while you sing
- Always keep going, even if you make a mistake

In the Shadows

Starting the Day

- Take the same step-by-step approach as for *In the Shadows* (above) – rhythm first, then notes in free time, then both together
- Note that this lively song is in the key of G, and that the second phrase is louder than the first

It Takes Two (continued)

- Always remember: rhythm first, then notes in free time, then both together – with expression marks too!

Gently Does It!

Bandstand

Autumn Landscape

It Takes Two (continued)

An Important Day

There and Back

By the Fireside

Workout 5

3/4

Copy the rhythm

- Echo this rhythm with your teacher by singing back each phrase in time, without looking at the music
- Your teacher will count in two bars ('1–2–3, 1–2–3') before starting
- You can both tap the beat throughout

Rhythm

Here are some rhythms in the new time signature 3/4 (three crotchet beats in each bar).

- Sing these phrases to any suitable syllable while tapping the beat
- Find the starting note, with your teacher's help if needed
- Remember to take a breath during the crotchet rest in the middle – but keep tapping the beat!

Workout 6

Singing back

- Make a tune with your teacher by echoing each phrase in time, without looking at the music
- Your teacher will play you the key-chord and first note, and count in two bars
- You can both tap the beat throughout

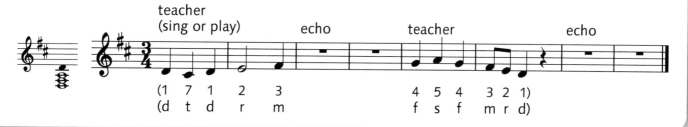

Rhythm and notes

These tunes in 3/4 time are in several different keys, still always starting and ending on the key-note.

- Check the key signature, and listen to the key-chord and starting note
- Sing the rhythm on the starting note only, while tapping the beat
- Then sing all the notes in free time
- Lastly, put rhythm and notes together, tapping the beat quietly throughout

Workout 7

Copy the rhythm

- Echo this rhythm with your teacher by singing back each phrase in time, without looking at the music
- Your teacher will count in two bars before starting
- You can both tap the beat throughout

Rhythm

These rhythms in 3/4 time now include dotted notes.

- Sing these phrases to any suitable syllable while tapping the beat
- Find the starting note, with your teacher's help if needed
- Remember to take a breath during the crotchet rest in the middle – but keep tapping the beat!

Workout 8

Singing back

- Make a tune with your teacher by echoing each phrase in time, without looking at the music
- Your teacher will play you the key-chord and first note, and count in two bars
- You can both tap the beat throughout

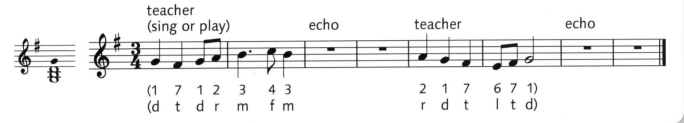

teacher (sing or play)   echo   teacher   echo

(1 7 1 2 3 4 3   2 1 7 6 7 1)
(d t d r m f m   r d t l t d)

Rhythm and notes

Here are some more tunes to sing in 3/4 time.

- Check the key signature, and listen to the key-chord and starting note
- Sing the rhythm on the starting note only, while tapping the beat
- Then sing all the notes in free time
- Lastly, put rhythm and notes together, tapping the beat quietly throughout

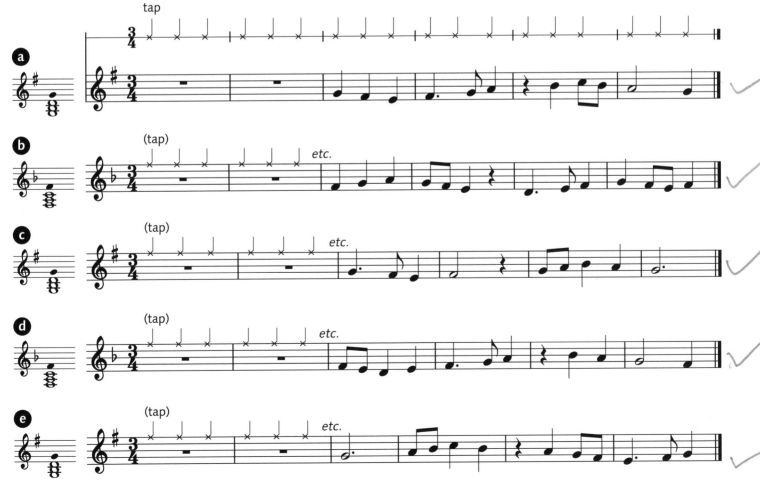

Make Music

Hot-Air Balloon

Make a song to fit the words below:
- First, say the words out loud to make a rhythm in 3/4 time
- Now make it into a song in the key of F major

Floating so high above the trees, gently swaying in the breeze.

Rolling Along

- Sing this rhythm on the note D several times, to any syllable
- Now make the rhythm into a tune in the key of D major

It Takes Two

Here are two more duets to sing with your teacher or another pupil, followed by three pages of songs for voice and piano.

Expressive Song

- Before you sing this duet, prepare it in the same way as for *Cloudless Landscape* on page 8 – rhythm first, then notes in free time, then rhythm and notes combined

After You...

- In this round, Voice 2 starts when Voice 1 reaches the ✱ sign
- Repeat several times, if you wish

It Takes Two (continued)

Prepare *Delicate Dance* like this:

- Check the time signature, tempo and key signature, and listen to the key-chord and starting note
- Sing the rhythm on the starting note only, while tapping the beat

- Then sing all the notes in free time – repeat until you are sure that they are right

- Now put rhythm and notes together
- Follow the expression marks and give the phrases a sense of flow
- When you are ready to sing with the piano, listen again to the key-chord and starting note, and tap two bars before you start – keep tapping quietly while you sing
- Always keep going, even if you make a mistake

Delicate Dance

Question and Answer

- Take the same step-by-step approach as for *Delicate Dance* (above)
- Note that this lively song is in the key of F, and that the 'answer' is louder than the 'question'!

It Takes Two (continued)

- Always remember: rhythm first, then notes in free time, then both together – with expression marks too!

Calm Waters

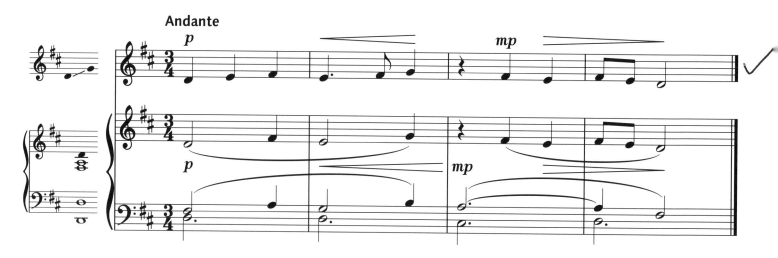

Cheerful Meeting

Morning Minuet

It Takes Two (continued)

Drifting

Waltz

Looking Around

Major keys

(rising only)

1   3
doh me

Singing back

- Make a tune with your teacher by echoing each phrase in time, in the same way as before

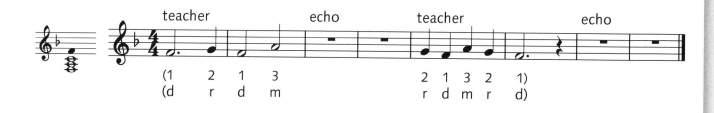

teacher   echo   teacher   echo

(1   2   1   3   2   1   3   2   1)
(d   r   d   m   r   d   m   r   d)

Rhythm and notes

The tunes on this page, and in the following Workouts, are in 4/4 or 3/4 time. Remember to check how many beats there are in the bar before you start, and tap the beat as quietly as you can.

Look out for the leaps of a 3rd! On this page, they are from the 1st note of the scale up to the 3rd note.

- Check the time signature and key signature, and listen to the key-chord and starting note
- As before, sing the rhythm on the starting note first, followed by all the notes in free time – then put rhythm and notes together

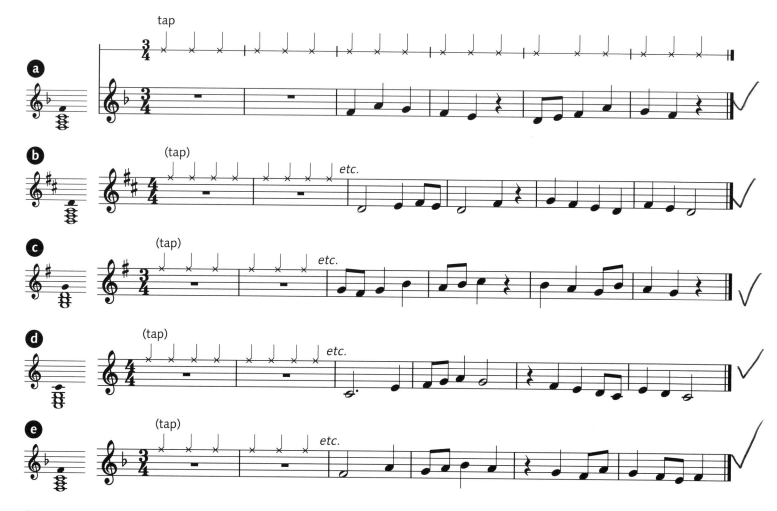

Workout 10

Major keys (rising only) 3 5 me soh

Singing back

- Make a tune with your teacher by echoing each phrase in time

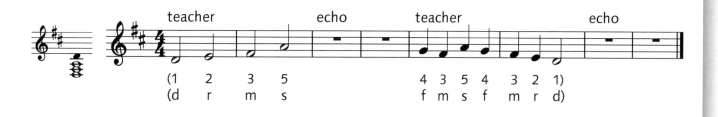

teacher   echo   teacher   echo

(1 2 3 5   4 3 5 4 3 2 1)
(d r m s   f m s f m r d)

Rhythm and notes

In these tunes, the leaps are still of a 3rd, but now from the 3rd to the 5th notes of the scale.

- Check the time signature and key signature, and listen to the key-chord and starting note
- Sing the rhythm on the starting note first, followed by all the notes in free time – then put rhythm and notes together

Workout 11

Singing back

- Make a tune with your teacher by echoing each phrase in time

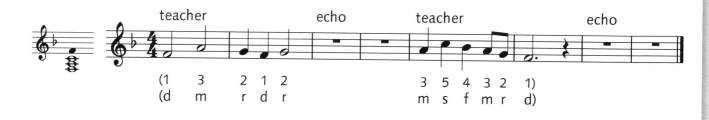

teacher   echo   teacher   echo

(1   3   2   1   2   3   5   4   3   2   1)
(d   m   r   d   r   m   s   f   m   r   d)

Rhythm and notes

The tunes on these two pages use both the leaps introduced in Workouts 9 and 10.

- Check the time signature and key signature, and listen to the key-chord and starting note
- Remember – rhythm first, then notes, then both together!

22

Workout 12

Major keys
1 3 — doh me
3 5 — me soh (rising only)

Singing back

- Make a tune with your teacher by echoing each phrase in time

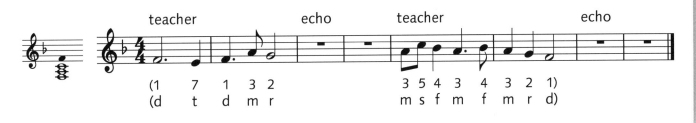

teacher   echo   teacher   echo

(1   7   1   3   2   3   5   4   3   4   3   2   1)
(d   t   d   m   r   m   s   f   m   f   m   r   d)

Rhythm and notes

These tunes have dotted rhythms as well as leaps.

- Check the time signature and key signature, and listen to the key-chord and starting note
- Remember – rhythm first, then notes, then both together!

23

Make Music

Surfing

Make a song to fit the words below:
- First, say the words out loud to make a rhythm in 4/4 or 3/4 time
- Now make it into a song in the key of D major

Blazing sun, shimmering haze, skimming on the breaking waves.

Hopping

- Sing this rhythm on the note G several times, to any syllable
- Now make the rhythm into a tune in the key of G major
- See if you can hop some 3rds!

It Takes Two

Here are two more duets to sing with your teacher or another pupil, followed by two songs for voice and piano.

Water Lilies

Remember:
- Rhythm first, then notes in free time, then rhythm and notes combined – then sing the duet together

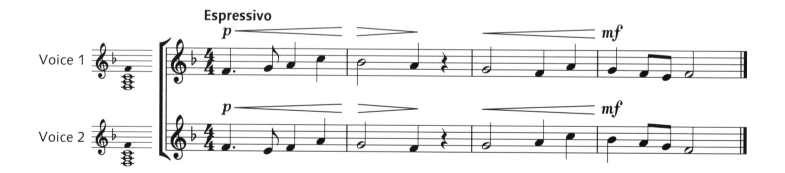

Morning Sunshine

- In this round, Voice 2 starts when Voice 1 reaches the ✱ sign
- Repeat several times, if you wish

It Takes Two (continued)

Prepare *Songbirds* like this:

- Check the time signature, tempo and key signature, and listen to the key-chord and starting note
- Sing the rhythm on the starting note only, while tapping the beat

- Then sing all the notes in free time – repeat until you are sure that they are right

- Now put rhythm and notes together
- Follow the expression marks – note the crescendo in both phrases
- When you are ready to sing with the piano, listen again to the key-chord and starting note, and tap two bars before you start – keep tapping quietly while you sing
- Always keep going, even if you make a mistake

Songbirds

Sweet Dreams

- Achieve the expressive feeling by gently shaping the crescendo and diminuendo hairpins

Read and Sing

Here are some more songs to practise sight-singing with piano, similar to the tests in the ABRSM Grade 2 Singing exam.

- Make sure you can sing the rhythm while tapping the beat
- Then sing the notes in free time, checking carefully for any leaps
- Now put rhythm and notes together, tapping two bars quietly before you begin
- Always remember to keep going in time with the piano, even if you make a mistake

Up and Down the Ladder

Distant Clouds

Merry-Go-Round

Read and Sing (continued)

Moonlight

Early Morning Stretch

Alpine Song

Read and Sing (continued)

Round the Corner

Sarabande

In the Valley

Cheerful Song

Graceful Dance

Diving Board

Read and Sing (continued)

Running Shoes

The Orchard

Solemn March

Read and Sing (continued)

For those who wish to practise reading both clefs, here are the songs from page 30, but now in the bass clef and transposed to different keys.

Running Shoes

The Orchard

Solemn March

Songs with Words

Here are two songs that you can learn to sing. The first can be sung by a group of singers, divided into up to eight parts; the second can be sung solo or by a group of singers, with piano.

On the River

- Learn this round by singing it all together first
- Then split into parts – any number from two to eight
- Each new part comes in when the previous part reaches the ✱ sign
- Sing it through as many times as you like!

Steps and Jumps

- Here's a song that explores steps of a 2nd and jumps of a 3rd